BEYOND LIMITATIONS

The Secret of Ruth's and Rahab's Visions

M. K. Komi

WestBow Press books may be ordered through booksellers or by contacting:

WestBow Press
A Division of Thomas Nelson & Zondervan
1663 Liberty Drive
Bloomington, IN 47403
www.westbowpress.com
1 (866) 928-1240

ISBN: 978-1-9736-4936-6 (sc)
ISBN: 978-1-9736-4935-9 (hc)
ISBN: 978-1-9736-4937-3 (e)

Library of Congress Control Number: 2018914892

Print information available on the last page.

WestBow Press rev. date: 12/31/2018

I would like to dedicate this book to my wife Lydie who has stood firm and faithful through the tough times I have endured. And also, I would like to express my deepest love for my three children Melchi, Gabrielle, and Perce for cheering me up through the process of writing this book. Thank you!

Contents

Introduction

The Bible was written for our instruction. It is a book of inspiration and impartation. Every story in it is written to show us the possibilities that we have in God. We can pick any story that is related to our present circumstance and apply the principle therein. The amazing thing is that we will experience the same result that the people in the Bible did. The truth of God as revealed in the Bible is timeless—even though, at the same time, it is timely. It has a historical background that applies to a specific time in history, but its message can be applied throughout every generation. The truth of God is living and effective. Its power is eternal.

Among those truths, I found two fascinating ones: the stories of Ruth and Rahab. For me, these two stories relate to many facets to the lives of people in different walks of life. These two women had challenges like ours. Their backgrounds disqualified them from having access to God's blessings. They came out of a nation that was cursed by God. Tragic events took place, which they had to face and survive in order to break the imposed limitations. They both risked their lives in some ways for the attainment of divine blessings. They both also reached the apex that defines greatness or failure—they reached a defining moment when significant choices had to be made. Through all those ordeals, they broke every barrier they faced, eventually establishing themselves through divine approval as great heroines of faith.

This means that the limitations we face, no matter their origin, can never be looked at as the end of our life journeys. We can go beyond the present realities, we can go beyond tragedies and face fire and high waters, and still come out on top. We can break limitations and reach our goals. We can climb high mountains, if we cannot move them, to reach the other side. We can be more than we are now. Nothing is impossible to those who believe.

The intent of this book is to survey the lives of Ruth and Rahab and find the timeless truth that set them free from their present realities and transformed them into icons of faith. Let us remember that God's truth is always timeless. The truth that proceeds from his Word delivers the same value wherever it is applied.

Part I
Ruth's Decree

The story of Ruth is one the most heroic tales ever told. I know we think of a hero as someone who has fought mighty battles or conquered armies. However, the kind of courage Ruth displayed is as heroic as fearlessly facing mighty armies. Her story is one of hope because it depicts a few fascinating elements:

- bouncing back from tremendous loss
- making definite choices when life throws its worst
- relocating from nowhere to be established somewhere
- coming from the backdrop of history to becoming an icon
- seeing and going beyond present limitations
- grasping all that one dreams about

Ruth's life changed dramatically, proving again that change is possible. We can change the present condition of our lives from worst to best. Ruth defied her past, faced her present, and eventually embraced a better future, proving that nothing is impossible to those who believe—to those who see with a higher and divine perspective.

However, something very peculiar was at the core of the change Ruth experienced. It was the starting point of breakthrough. The key to such a possible turnaround is found in Ruth's statement to Naomi:

> "Look," said Naomi, "your sister-in-law is going back to her people and her gods. Go

back with her." But Ruth replied, "Don't urge me to leave you or to turn back from you. Where you go I will go, and where you stay I will stay. Your people will be my people and your God my God. Where you die I will die, and there I will be buried. May the Lord deal with me, be it ever so severely, if even death separates you and me." When Naomi realized that Ruth was determined to go with her, she stopped urging her. (Ruth 1:15–18 NIV)

In this passage, Ruth makes five powerful promises:

1. Where you go, I will go.
2. Where you stay, I will stay.
3. Your people will be my people.
4. Your God will be my God.
5. Where you die, I will die.

These promises are game changers in Ruth's life and destiny. Everything that comes after—the blessings, the changes, and the divine grafting into the messianic lineage—is a result of these simple yet powerful statements.

1
Where You Go, I Will Go

Destiny Requires that One Know the Destination

Where do you want to go? Unless you answer this question properly, moving forward becomes difficult or practically impossible. If we have not clearly determined where we want to go in life, even our present position is uncertain. Today we must determine our tomorrow and where we want to go. This is the cue of every vision—defining where we would like to move next.

Vision contains the possibility to become. God has already promised us that whatever we see, we can possess. Remember what God said to Abraham: "And the Lord said to Abram, after Lot had separated from him: 'Lift your eyes now and look from the place where you are—northward, southward, eastward, and westward; for all the land which you see I give to you and your descendants forever'" (Gen. 13:14–15 NKJV).

Notice that God came to Abraham at a very painful

time—after Lot had separated from him. There were reasons why God came in that moment to speak to Abraham and activate a vision in his heart. You know first that they were in a strange country. There is always relief not to be alone in a foreign land. Lot was a great comfort to Abraham; he was like Abraham's only son, although Lot was Abraham's nephew. Not having any child at that time, Abraham probably had a lot of hope in this young man.

After having shared so many experiences and moved together with a common purpose, Lot abruptly walked away from Abraham in a foreign land. This was a shock for Abraham. Often it is in moments of separation that people lose their vision for the future. We have the tendency to think that those who have left us have taken our futures with them, because we have put so much hope in them. Loss can feel like it cripples our dreams.

God came to Abraham at that place and told him not to look down, but to lift his eyes from loss and separation and dream again. God told Abraham to walk from that place and keep moving.

Ruth had the same dilemma; she had lost so much. But instead of walking away, like Orpah, she lifted her eyes and saw Bethlehem. She decided that the present loss would never stop her from going somewhere. She dared to dream for something. That simple moment shifted everything in her eternal destiny.

You cannot excuse yourself from destiny or from every prior dream you had because of a present loss. What is lost is lost. The future contains greater promises than today. All it takes to achieve that promise is for you to shake off the dust and decide where you want to go. You can decide to move forward.

Look at David at Ziklag. Upon their return to the city, David and his men of war found out that the Amalekites had raided the city and taken captive everyone after burning it to the ground. The sorrow was so great that the Bible shows how the soldiers who were with David cried till they had no strength left in them. They focused their anger toward David and tried to stone him.

David did not allow this event to stop him. He inquired of the Lord whether he could pursue (1 Sam. 30:1–8). David looked forward, not backward—and the Lord told him that if he pursued, he would surely overtake the enemy and recover all.

Our very existence is in limbo if we lack vision. In a sense, when we take hold of a very defined and specific vision, we take our lives into our own hands. This does not mean that God is put out of the equation. In fact, God wants us to take charge so that his Spirit will come alongside to hold the other parts of our lives, helping us accomplish the goals we have laid out. But the crucial question is still: where do you want to go?

I believe that the difference between successful and unsuccessful people lies in this simple fact—that successful people have dared to dream big. They knew exactly where they wanted to go and what they wanted to accomplish. Unsuccessful people were perhaps blinded by present realities and thus lacked a proper vision for the future.

The plan of God for our lives depends on vision or hope for the future. Look carefully in Jeremiah 29:11: "'For I know the plans I have for you,' declares the LORD, 'plans to prosper you and not to harm you, plans to give you hope and a future.'" Hope and a future are given to us in the form of a vision that we must be able to see, recognize, and pursue. We are the sole deciders of our destinies.

Our vision helps us know our whereabouts in life. It helps us connect with the right people and be in the right place at the right moment. It helps us step into our seasons on time. When our vision is very precise, opportunities become very visible. Right connections are easily detected, and life is full of meaning and purpose.

With the knowledge of where we want to go, we cease being victims of someone else's decisions or someone else's anger. It is time to stand up and move. Decide today where you want to go. The world is full of many places you can go, many people you can connect to, and many things you can do. There is so much you can become. This time requires that you decide once and for all where you want to go.

To Know Where You Are Going, You Must Know Where You Are

You cannot decide where you want to go unless you define your present position. You cannot decide to grow unless you know where you are currently. Blindness to your present state robs you of the desire to move into greater exploits in life. No one can guide you to where you want to go when you are lost—unless you locate where you are.

If you are lost on a freeway, you may ask me, "Hey, I am lost," or "Hey, I cannot find this address, can you help me?"

The first question I will ask you in return is "Where are you?" If you cannot tell me where you are, I cannot help you. Knowing where you are makes it much easier to know where you want to go in life.

Is the state you are now in satisfying? If you are dissatisfied with where you are, and if you believe that you were made for more, then it is time for you to define where you want to go.

Remember that everything in the world around you has been placed there to help you define where you are. When I ask you where you are, your first reaction will be to look around you. You will try to find a sign in your surroundings to tell where you are. How do you define where you are right now in your life?

This was the very first question God asked man after the fall (Gen. 3:9). The question "Where are you?" has a redemptive tone. If you want to redeem your life, buy back your honor, and find your rightful place, you must answer this redemptive question.

To know where you are is connected to clearly knowing where you are supposed to go. A lucid vision lets us know how much effort we need to make to move forward. It shows us whether we are running slow or not. It helps us know when to stop to get the necessary resources for the journey ahead. Vision is the ultimate key for knowing our present position in life.

Do you know clearly where you are supposed to go? Do you know who you want to become? Do you know what you want to achieve? Have you made a detailed plan to fulfill your vision?

Once you identify where you are, you will be able to decide whether you have to restart, continue, or maintain the same pace. You will also see whether you will allow those signs to fuel your heart for greater achievements.

What You Pursue Defines What You Are Entitled to Possess

You are not entitled to possess or access what you don't have the guts to pursue. Good fortune is not given to all, only to those who dare to pursue something. Only those who dare to dream of going somewhere in life will find such fortune. Those who pursue nothing will possess nothing. God told David, "Pursue: for thou shalt surely overtake them, and without fail recover all" (1 Sam. 30:8 KJV).

Are we ready to pursue and recover the dignity we have lost, the time we have lost? Ruth was brave enough to rise from the ashes of life's tragedies and persevere. Even when she went to Bethlehem, she set her eyes on the harvest with faith that she would find favor along the way. You see, favor is not random; favor is grasped by dream chasers. Favor is for those who decide not to let what happens in life to stop them. Favor is for those who decide to go somewhere, for those who are living to pursue their God-given passion. These are the ones who live constantly under the flow of God's favor. It will find them at every corner and in any field they might be.

The Willingness to Become Is Key to Success

Ruth was willing to go somewhere. She was determined to become who God had intended for her to become. Such desire is what the Enemy steals from people. The possibility to become has been given to us by God. God has given us all the power and will to decide what we want to do. To the same degree that we can decide to do evil, we are also capable of deciding to do good. We decide our fate in life.

I don't believe that men or the Devil have enough power to stop us from doing what we want to do. Yet lack of courage makes us the prey of human will. The fulfilment of destiny and dreams demands courage. Look at Joshua; God gave him such wonderful promises, as we read in the Bible.

After the death of Moses the servant of the Lord, it came to pass that the Lord spoke to Joshua the son of Nun, Moses' assistant, saying: "Moses My servant is dead. Now therefore, arise, go over this Jordan, you and all this people, to the land which I am giving to them—the children of Israel. Every place that the sole of your foot will tread upon I have given you, as I said to Moses. From the wilderness and this Lebanon as far as the great river, the River Euphrates, all the land of the Hittites, and to the Great Sea toward the going down of the sun, shall be your territory. No man shall be able to stand before you all the days of your life; as I was with Moses, so I will be with you. I will not leave you nor forsake you. Be strong and of good courage, for to this people you shall divide as an inheritance the land which I swore to their fathers to give them. Only be strong and very courageous, that you may observe to do according to all the law which Moses My servant commanded you; do not turn from it to the right hand or to the left, that you may prosper wherever you go. (Josh. 1:1–8 NKJV)

Notice that God first reminded Joshua of the death of

Moses. This shows that Joshua was locked up in a place of grief, living in the memory of loss. Moses's death paralyzed Joshua's ability to move forward. He could not believe it and was somewhat living in a state of denial. Thus, God reminded him that Moses was dead, and there was nothing else to do but rise and move forward.

Joshua received powerful promises. In return, God told him to be courageous. God told Joshua no one would stand before him as long as he lived, for God would be with him. There would be no mountain so high that Joshua couldn't climb it, no giant tall enough that Joshua couldn't destroy it. He had the promise and the Promisor with him. But God told Joshua that having the promises was one thing, and being of good courage was another. This meant that the only enemy Joshua would have to defeat with his own will was discouragement.

People can criticize us, the Devil can attack us, and society can squeeze us, but at the end of the day, the decision to pursue or quit is ours. Are you willing to pursue? Do you have the courage to face day and night, winds and waves, setbacks and unfairness to pursue what is burning in your heart?

Pursuing what we want in life does not exclude weariness. The weight of life's demands will be at many points unbearable. Sometimes weariness will come because of the delay of what we are hoping for. Indeed, many people give up, not because of the uncertainty of their hopes, but just because of the delay. Because they have waited for so long and the breakthrough did not happen, they decide to give up.

Breakthrough in destiny demands resilience. It takes some fortitude to see dreams happen. Gideon is a good example to demonstrate that we are still called to keep on pressing, even when the going gets tough. "When Gideon came to the Jordan, he and the three hundred men who were with him crossed over, exhausted but still in pursuit" (Judg. 8:4 NKJV).

The fulfillment of all that we hope for will require patience, for it is through faith and patience that promises are delivered to us. Despite ongoing conflict and opposition we will face, nothing will make our dreams untrue unless we give up. Conflicts and delay do not make dreams untrue. If properly handled, they will eventually fuel our capacity to press on toward the prize.

Nothing will make our dreams untrue unless we give up.

The Passion Behind Your Vision Is a Great Asset for Success

Having a vision for your future is the starting point, but what makes vision come true is the passion we possess. Ruth was a woman of passion. She knew how to cling to and pursue what she wanted to have. Her resilience was fueled by a deep yearning within, such that she could stand almost all day in Boaz's field. Passion is that thing you can't live without.

It must happen. It is the thought, *I have got to get it; I must accomplish it.* That is the tone of passion.

I have seen a lot of people with tremendous potential, yet they ended up failing in life because they lacked passion. Your potential is not your destiny, only an asset for achieving greatness. Your passion is the driving force that pushes your boat into your tomorrow. The question is, how bad do you want it?

The difference between people is not in the potential they possess, but the passion they put behind what they do. Every person is endowed with natural potential. Passion is what makes the difference.

Passion also helps identify God's agenda for you. As a child of God, your pure passion is an indication of God's present program for you. It defines the season you have stepped into. Not to follow such passion is to miss God's plan for your life. In consequence, you miss the mark of divine opportunities in a life season. What is your heart beating the most for?

If You Can Swim in an Uncomfortable Place, You Are Already a Winner

A great visionary who wants to go somewhere must be ready to go to uncomfortable places. Ruth's breakthrough came because she was not afraid to go to an unfamiliar place. It was not easy for her. Imagine a Moabite among the Israelites. That was an uncomfortable situation. Her greater blessings sprang from such uncomfortable places. If you want to go somewhere, be prepared to walk through uncomfortable places, for it is through those places that your gift will shine the most.

Ruth was placed behind the reapers— a very unfavorable position—but it did not matter (Ruth 2:6–7). She set her eyes on a great tomorrow. She pursued something she knew was possible. It did not matter where she was placed—it was only a matter of time before her gift made a place for her.

Just because we start low does not mean that we will remain there. Small beginnings do not suggest failure. If we have passion and full commitment to the cause, eventually a path will be created for us to find our place of honor and influence in life.

2
Where You Dwell, I Will Dwell

The second promise of Ruth was around the dwelling place. Where do you desire to dwell? To be productive in life and move into a place of greatness, we must decide where we want to dwell. There are two implications here. First, our dwelling place is in Christ. Second, we must refuse to dwell in the past. We must be focused now on our hope of the future that God has placed within us.

Dwelling and Abiding in His Presence

The Lord clearly revealed to us the secret for producing fruits in life. In John 15 the Lord states:

> I am the true vine, and My Father is the vinedresser. Every branch in Me that does not bear fruit, He takes away; and every branch that bears fruit, He prunes it so that it may bear more fruit. You are already clean because

of the word which I have spoken to you. Abide in Me, and I in you. As the branch, cannot bear fruit of itself unless it abides in the vine, so neither can you unless you abide in Me. I am the vine, you are the branches; he who abides in Me and I in him, he bears much fruit, for apart from Me you can do nothing. If anyone does not abide in Me, he is thrown away as a branch and dries up; and they gather them, and cast them into the fire and they are burned. If you abide in Me, and My words abide in you, ask whatever you wish, and it will be done for you. (John 15:1–7 NKJV)

The abiding life is the key to producing fruits in all we are doing in life. As believers, there is no way we can produce fruits that please God the Father unless we abide in Christ by abiding by his words. There is success in life that comes through worldly philosophy; such success will be but building a tower of Babel—a tower of confusion that will crumble one day. Everything that humanity builds by their own strength without God's input is a tower of Babel and confusion.

Without God, our strength is as much a handicap as our weakness, and our wisdom is as much a handicap as our folly and ignorance. Look at the world in its success without God. Our goal in life should be to live closer to God as we pursue the dreams and passions he placed in our hearts.

Our greatest good and achievement should be God, not our dreams. Your dream and vision are supposed to create a path for God to be known more in this world.

Ruth's blessing was not for herself, but became a conducive path for God to reveal his Son to mankind. So were Abraham's lifespan and blessings, and all the great men and women who lived as seen in the Bible, abiding under the shelter of the Most High. "He who dwells in the shelter of the Most High shall abide in the shadow of the Almighty—I say of the Lord" (Ps. 91:1 NASB). This passage is interesting. We may not grasp its true meaning unless we translate the divine names in Hebrew, so that it reads as follows: "He who dwells in the secret place of El-Elyon shall abide in the shadow of El Shaddai—I say of Adonai you are my God." We see in the abiding life three names associated with God—El Elyon, El-Shaddai, and Adonai.

To dwell in the shelter of El Elyon means to live in communion with God through the Holy Spirit. The first mention of the name El Elyon is in Genesis 14:18, in relation to Melchizedek. He is presented as the priest of God Most High or El Elyon. So we see that the name is attached to the priesthood, which is understood as the service of worship, praise, thanksgiving, and prayers to God. Priesthood points to our intimate communion with God.

We also know that when Melchizedek came to Abraham, Melchizedek brought Abraham bread and wine. In John chapter 6, Christ spoke about drinking the wine of his blood and eating the bread of his flesh as the only way one can truly walk with God (John 6:53–58). The bread and wine spoke of communion with him and the Father.

El Shaddai means "God all sufficient." The name was revealed to Abraham after the birth of Ishmael. The instruction attached to that name was that Abraham had to walk before God and be blameless (Gen. 17:1). This means that in the abiding life, we need to live in continuous communion with God, walk before him, and remain blameless. The power of communion is the communicator of every possible and needed grace to walk before God and be blameless. In doing so, we will know God as Adonai, the Master, a name revealed to Abraham in Genesis 15:1–2, when God told Abraham that he was Abraham's shield and that Abraham's reward would be great.

The wonderful thing I discovered is that John 6 reveals all three attributes of the Father in Christ. Jesus multiplied the loaves, revealing that he is all-sufficient. Jesus asked his disciples to drink his blood and eat his flesh, introducing himself as the communion of El-Elyon. And later Jesus asked them to follow him, which means he is Adonai, the Master.

The safest place to be in this world is in the presence of God. The safest way to walk is to walk before the presence of God. As we learn to abide through daily communion, we will tap into the abundant life Christ gave. Let us remember that how close we live to God here on earth will determine how close we will be with him in eternity. Our present relationship with God and present communion with him determine our eternal placement.

When Ruth came to dwell in Bethlehem, she was told that she came under the wings of the God of Israel. She found her dwelling place under his wings. "May the Lord reward your work, and your wages be full from the Lord, the God of Israel, under whose wings you have come to seek refuge" (Ruth 2:12 NASB).

Jesus said, "If anyone serves Me, let him follow Me; and where I am, there My servant will be also. If anyone serves Me, him My Father will honor" (John 12:26 NASB).

Dwelling in the Future

Our past can have such bearing on us to the point that we can become afraid of the future. Many have not dared step into their future because they have been caught up in their past failures, past mistakes, or past tragedies. It would have been easy for Ruth to let yesterday's tragedies stop her from moving forward. In fact, she had more affliction and disappointments than we could ever imagine. She married a guy and he died; her father-in-law also died; and she was unable to bear a child. She had reasons to be trapped in those seeming failures. There was no apparent reason for her to move to Bethlehem, her future. But she disregarded those tragedies and decided to look forward.

Do you know how many people have buried their

tomorrows yesterday? Do you know how many people are still mourning over what is already past? They can't see the future God has for them. Do you know how many people are in despair because of what happened yesterday? They cannot embrace today the hope for the future God is giving them.

Do we know why one thief on the cross was saved and the other was lost forever? The answer is, the lost one was focused on the past. He was trapped in what he had done yesterday and how he had failed yesterday. The other was focused on the future. Look at the account as Scripture shows:

> One of the criminals who were hanged there was hurling abuse at Him, saying, "Are You not the Christ? Save Yourself and us!" But the other answered, and rebuking him said, "Do you not even fear God, since you are under the same sentence of condemnation? And we indeed are suffering justly, for we are receiving what we deserve for our deeds; but this man has done nothing wrong." And he was saying, "Jesus, remember me when You come in Your kingdom!" And He said to him, "Truly I say to you, today you shall be with Me in Paradise." (Luke 23:39–43 NASB)

The first thief was so locked in the past that he used abusive words to denigrate the greatness of Christ. You'll notice he saw Christ in the light of his own prejudice. He lowered Christ to his level and looked at Christ as a sinner.

The other thief considered the future and refused to be locked in his past. He did not look at Christ based on his own prejudice. In his confession, we see a tremendous desire to experience the future. He told Christ, "Remember me when you come in your kingdom." In this statement, we see a load of truth.

First, they were about to die—all three of them. But the thief who was saved saw beyond death. He saw Jesus being alive. Not only did he see life after death, but he spoke of the messianic kingdom: He saw the kingdom of God and saw Christ as the King. Wow! What a vision. Hanging on the cross, he nevertheless saw resurrection, life, the King, and the kingdom, and believed in the possibility of living again. In that moment, Jesus told him that his future was not tomorrow—it began that same evening.

Many have been in a position of the crucified thieves. We have come to the end of our lives with nowhere on earth left to go. Often it is here that we become indifferent to God and his promises. But with God, the possibility is beyond. Our end or our extremity is God's opportunity. What we see in those moments with God is our only way out. If we dwell in our pain and let it dictate the present, we will lose hold of our appointment with destiny. Every time we let past and present circumstances control our lives, we lose something in the future. The future of every human being is not truly in front of but inside them—and the future is always the future present. Christ said, "But the hour is coming, and now is" (John 4:23 NKJV). This is a future present reality. This means you can step into your future in a few weeks or a few months. But such a future is only activated if we refuse to live in the past and claim our future in God.

There is another story showing how the past can corrupt our present and kill our future.

> Terah lived seventy years, and became the father of Abram, Nahor and Haran.
>
> Now these are the records of the generations of Terah. Terah became the father of Abram, Nahor and Haran; and Haran became the father of Lot. Haran died in the presence of his father Terah in the land of his birth, in Ur of the Chaldeans. Abram and Nah.or took wives for themselves. The name of Abram's wife was Sarai; and the name of Nahor's wife was Milcah, the daughter of Haran, the father of Milcah and Iscah. Sarai was barren; she had no child.
>
> Terah took Abram his son, and Lot the son of Haran, his grandson, and Sarai his daughter-in-law, his son Abram's wife; and they went out together from Ur of the Chaldeans in order to enter the land of Canaan; and they went as far

as Haran, and settled there. The days of Terah were two hundred and five years; and Terah died in Haran." (Gen. 11:26–32 NASB)

Notice that Terah's youngest son, Haran, died in the presence of his father. For the Bible to state such a tragedy in such fashion shows that it was a shock to Terah. He lost his youngest son, and that was more than someone could ever handle. But the tragedy did not stop him from taking his family to Canaan, the land promised to Abraham. He decided to forge towards the future.

However, the Bible shows that along the way, they stopped in a city named Haran. Terah died in Haran. I strongly believe that the city reminded him of what he had lost in the past. It awakened the memory of past loss, and from there he couldn't go further. The memory of the past cut him off from the promise given to Abraham. In fact, the past was so entrenched in this family that even Abraham could not move from there. Scripture shows that it took a divine intervention to move him out of Haran (Acts 7:4).

What was been done against you is less than what has been done for you. Your failures in the past are nothing compared to your hope for the future.

What is your Haran? What is the past that is keeping you from your future? Don't let yesterday's abuses keep you from enjoying your life the way God wants you to. Do not sell your future in God because of what someone has done against you—or because of what you lost yesterday. This is the time you must choose to dwell in the hope for the future. No one can reach to the future if one is holding on to one's past. Paul clearly states that the way to take hold of the great prize is to forget what lies behind: "But one thing I do: forgetting what lies behind and reaching forward to what lies ahead" (Phil. 3:13 NASB).

Ruth could have gone back to Moab, like Orpah, and disappeared forever, but she refused to. She pressed forward.

It's Never Too Late to Embrace Your Hope for the Future

There are those who have given up because they look at the time they have wasted. They regret where they are. Let me ask you a question. If God turned your clock back twenty years, what would you do?

Many say they would go back to school. Some say they would save money and plan carefully to avoid their present situation. Others say they would have tried harness their passion for a business. It is never too late to fulfill those dreams; all you must do is reset now.

Listen, the very fact that you are alive is enough proof that you have been given a second chance to make things right. I believe you are always living in your Kairos moment, to see things change for the best. As long as you live, there is still hope.

3

Your People Will Be My People

When Ruth embraced the people of Naomi, she broke a culture barrier. The Hebrew people spoke another language. They had another culture, another mind-set, another way of doing things. The only way Ruth could step into her destiny was to accept and embrace a new culture, a new mind-set, a new way of living, a new language, and even new apparel.

Breaking the Culture Barrier

One of the greatest barriers that hinders people from stepping into their destiny is the culture barrier. The contentment of keeping their own ways, their own mind-set, and their own way of speaking has limited them from achieving greatness in God. Culture involves a range of things, such as art, apparel, religion, music, laws, language, and food.

Breaking the culture barrier was imperative if Ruth was to reach the level of prominence she reached. She had to go against her own way of living and thinking, adopting another way of life. This did not by any means require compromising her values. It meant embracing the good part of the world she wanted to impact, while keeping her fundamental values.

A culture is group's set of beliefs, customs, behaviors, and ways of thinking. In this present world, as we aim to fulfill our God-given dreams, we must be flexible, adopting certain aspects of the culture of the domain we are trying to embrace.

Look at Daniel the prophet. God predestined him to walk in greatness, rule in the highest courts of Babylon, and rise up to the highest rank of both the Babylonian kingdom and the Medo-Persian kingdom. But to reach that place, he had to be educated according to the culture of Babylon, knowing their laws, customs, and languages.

> Young men in whom there was no blemish, but good-looking, gifted in all wisdom, possessing knowledge and quick to understand, who had ability to serve in the king's palace, and whom they might teach the language and literature of the Chaldeans. And the king appointed for them a daily provision of the king's delicacies and of the wine which he drank, and three years of training for them, so that at the end of that time they might serve before the king. Now from among those of the sons of Judah

were Daniel, Hananiah, Mishael, and Azariah.
(Dan. 1:4–6 NKJV)

Daniel and his friends had to be educated in and adopt the culture of the Babylonians before reigning therein. You need to know the culture you want to impact. You must have proper knowledge of the culture of business if you are to rule in the business world. You must have a proper knowledge of the culture of politics if you want to rule politically.

The church can never break through the higher courts of the world and destroy their idols unless she clearly understands the culture that drives the world. To say this is not to suggest that we compromise our values and standards as believers. It simply means we incarnate what we want to change and transform. The might of a king is the force to adapt without compromising. Paul had to behave like a Greek in order to win Greek souls, without compromising his faith and walk with God. He adapted to their ways of living; he embraced their culture, ate their food, understood who they were and how they thought in order to proclaim a kingdom and a culture greater than theirs. "And to the Jews I became as a Jew, that I might win Jews; to those who are under the law, as under the law, that I might win those who are under the law" (1 Cor. 9:20 NKJV).

Embracing a culture is a call to become expert in the language and way of behaving in places where God has set us to rule. In the plan of God, Ruth was called to rule, but such a plan could only be possible if she was ready to embrace a culture. We cannot operate successfully unless we understand the demands of cultures in different venues of human activities. This requires extensive research and contact with the world we are aiming at.

The Kingdom Culture—The Superior

The kingdom of God is real. It is more real than the kingdom of this world. The world kingdom is temporary, but God's kingdom is eternal. Whenever the kingdom of God collides with the kingdom of this world, or any other kingdom, it overpowers them.

Jesus demonstrated the kingdom of God when he walked the earth. He could subject everything, heal the sick, raise the dead, forgive sins, cleanse lepers, and multiply food to supply the need of the people. The kingdom of God is the realm of every supply, for it is the source of everything created.

While the world does not recognize its presence, we believers were saved and transferred by the divine act into this kingdom (Col. 1:13). We belong to the kingdom of God; we are citizens of the kingdom, and we are indeed children of the kingdom. The apostle Paul wrote that we are called to share in the inheritance of the saints in the kingdom of God.

However, like any kingdom, we must embrace the culture. A clear understanding of what God's kingdom is and how we must carry it out in our daily living is imperative for seeing greater breakthrough in our earthly realm.

In embracing the people of Naomi, Ruth embraced a kingdom, and the breakthrough she experienced later was according to the culture of the land. She had to operate according to those customs.

Repentance, not merely conversion, is the unlocking key to the culture of God's kingdom. Christ preached that we should repent, for the kingdom of God is at hand, meaning that access to the reality of God's kingdom demands repentance.

It should be noted that repentance does not mean simply giving up our sinful ways, even though such an idea is included in what repentance means. However, at its root, repentance is a change of mind. A transformed mind does not conform to the way of the world. It ushers a person into a tangible experience of the kingdom of God—by principle. Repentance is not only giving up our sin mind-set, it is also embracing the way of the kingdom.

It is to the degree that we allow our minds to be transformed that we will begin experiencing greater breakthrough. The kingdom of God breaks human limitations. When we are perfectly experiencing the kingdom of God in our lives, God's perfect will is done everywhere in our sphere of existence. Impossibilities become possibilities. Giants easily fall. Mountains are moved quickly and miracles happen. All these are possible only when we embrace the culture of this kingdom through a transformed mind—which is embracing and operating in the mind of Christ.

When our mind is truly transformed, the impossibilities that once drew us in can look very simple and logical.

Who Are Your People?

Who are your people? Which group do you belong to? Who is your mentor?

Ruth's statement that "your people will be my people" denotes the law of divine connection. Though your future is within you, nevertheless it is contained in the kind of relationships you share. No person succeeds alone. God will connect us with people with whom we will share a common destiny. We can easily be thwarted from our destiny if we embrace the wrong people. Bad company corrupts good manners. When Ruth promised to embrace the people of Naomi, she automatically grafted herself to the blessings that ran through this people. Fortunately for her, Israel was under Abrahamic blessings.

A great number of people have failed simply because they joined with the wrong people and wrong crowd. Every good vision (Reuben) that we hear from God (Simeon) must be joined (Levi) with good people or placed under a good mentor. Our destiny in God is precious, and we cannot afford to place it among wrong people.

Every relationship we bring into our lives will either add

or subtract something—there are no neutral relationships. There are also some relationships that may look good but are not suitable for us. Not every good person is supposed to join in what you are trying to birth. There must be discernment that enables us to choose the good people around us.

Who Is Your Naomi?

Not only does God give us or place us among good people, he also gives us mentors. For Ruth, the mentor was Naomi. Who is your Naomi? God can never connect you to Boaz unless you learn to submit to the Naomi he gave you. And it's possible Naomi will at times be very bitter (Ruth 1:20). Still, we are required to stay under our Naomi and follow her voice.

A person without a mentor can never go far. Scores of people did not break through in life not because of lack of potential or passion, but simply because they did not trust their mentors. Before we serve fully in our place of calling, we must learn to serve God before man. God will never call us his servant until we have successfully been the servant of another person.

Look at the life of Samuel. The Bible states that at the beginning of his journey to his calling, Samuel was ministering before the Lord (1 Sam. 2:18). Then Scripture says Samuel was ministering to the Lord *before Eli* (1 Sam. 3:1). Later, he stepped into his calling (1 Sam. 4:1).

Even Joshua was called *servant of Moses* before he was called *servant of God.* Elisha had to serve Elijah before he could be trusted to serve the Lord in his own office. I strongly believe that one who has not been faithful in serving under another will never be able to serve God. That is why God places us under a Naomi—to prove our worth in his enterprise.

Lack of guidance is one of the main sources of limitation in life. Whatever we are going through, someone has already been through it and has mastered it. We can find those people in person, through their writings, and through other means.

Why has the Lord placed shepherds in the church? It is so the shepherds can facilitate growth and help God's people walk in the steps the Lord has ordered for them. These leaders are placed in the lives of everyone called by God.

Mentorship is necessary, for through it we learn to borrow from other people's experiences. The link between Ruth and Boaz was Naomi. It was not Ruth's relationship that set her for life. Rather, it was Naomi's connection. The secret is that every leader and mentor is connected to a greater divine reality. They may not themselves walk into that realm and capacity, but they carry the deposit of greatness. Once you connect and submit to them, you set yourself up for greatness.

4

Your God Will Be My God

Ruth told Naomi that not only would Naomi's people be her people, but Naomi's God would be her God. This, I believe, was the most powerful statements of all her five statements. Behind this promise was hidden one of the most powerful truths. You see, it was not a simple thing to desire the God of Naomi. Generally, in the logic of things, concrete proof is required to convince someone to embrace another person's belief. By this I mean that I will adhere to your faith and believe in your God if I see proof of the goodness and the greatness of God over you.

It was a crazy thing for Ruth to believe in the God of Naomi. The things these women had gone through did not broadcast the glory of this God. Judging the chain of events from beginning to end, Naomi's God was not impressive.

Let us examine him from a clear perspective. From the very start, Bethlehem was in deep famine. The house of bread was in bad shape. God, who was supposed to be the Provider, was not providing. So Naomi and her family moved to Moab, and there she lost her husband. The God who had promised to protect the people of Judah did not protect. Her two sons married, and it seemed clear that her daughters-in-law could not conceive and give birth. The God of Naomi was unable to break barrenness. Then Naomi received another blow—her two sons died.

This woman clearly had nothing that reflected the goodness, power, care, and presence of God. In fact, in our modern time, she would be looked at as accursed by God. However, Ruth could see behind the broken life of Naomi, behind the embitterment brought about by life's realities. Ruth was able to see a God greater than the gods of Moab, and she made her claim. In a sense she told Naomi, "I see God in you. I see beyond your broken life. I see beyond your messes. I see God in his glory and power, and I want that God."

This was one of the most powerful statements of faith ever made. In its prophetic depth, it had a messianic mark. Ruth believed in the God of Naomi the same way the world had to believe in the God of Jesus. Jesus came into this world having been stripped of his radiant majesty. "Who has believed our report? And to whom has the arm of the Lord been revealed? For He shall grow up before Him as a tender plant, And as a root out of dry ground. He has no form or comeliness; And when we see Him, there is no beauty that we should desire Him. He is despised and rejected by men, A Man of sorrows and acquainted with grief" (Isa. 53:1–3 NKJV).

It's amazing that in the same way a Moabite came to believe in the God of Naomi, the nations came to believe in the Father of our Lord Jesus Christ. Behind Jesus's life on earth—where the glory of divinity was veiled with humanity—nations saw that he was the Son of God, the Source of eternal life.

Ruth's faith resonated from earth to heaven. It set the tone for something greater. The broken things of life are not the end of reality—they do not constitute all the reality of life that we have seen. Behind life's toughest issues, we can find God. God is not only hidden in beauty, but in ugliness. He is not only hidden in the light, but he indwells also in darkness. No matter where life issues have brought us, we can find God everywhere. David knew this and said: "Where can I go from Your Spirit? Or where can I flee from Your presence? If I ascend into heaven, You are there; If I make my bed in hell, behold, You are there" (Ps. 139:7–8 NKJV).

Beyond Broken Things

Breaking limitations requires that we see beyond the broken things of life. Life issues, disappointments, afflictions, tragedies, loss, and many other circumstances can build a wall of limitations in life, to the point that we find it difficult to make inroads. To move forward, we must develop a vision-faith that sees God.

When faced with limitations, it is difficult to see beyond.

Scores of people have killed their destinies at those tough moments. However, regardless of what we face, there is a truth that is undeniable—God is beyond everything we go through in life. We can decide to limit our vision to the calamities we face, or we can choose to see God. And surely, we will see him. God is the One who makes all things work together for the good of those who love him (Rom. 8:28).

In a broken world, we need more than our eyes to see. A clear spiritual perception enables us to see not only our current situation, but to look through and find the mind of God. God stands tall, and he alone is the Omega. *He* is the last—not our problems in life. Ruth chose to set her eyes on God, to grasp the wisdom of his mind. This was the harbinger of greatness.

In life, it is not what has happened to us that will deeply affect our destiny. Instead, it is what we decide to do afterward. The aftermath is where our life course is decided. Where will you go from here? The possibility of rising from the ashes of life is greater than the comfort or fear to remain where we have been hurt. When we learn to see God beyond, we will break limitations.

In Ziklag, David was depressed internally and he was oppressed externally. As a friend once pointed out, David turned to the Eternal (1 Sam. 30:6). David did not allow the circumstance to cripple him. He inquired of the Lord if he could pursue—meaning that David would press forward despite the present tragedy (1 Sam. 30:8).

Angels in the presence of the Lord worship and say powerful things. In his first great prophetic experience, Isaiah the prophet recounts: "In the year that King Uzziah died, I saw the Lord sitting on a throne, high and lifted up, and the train of His robe filled the temple. Above it stood seraphim; each one had six wings: with two he covered his face, with two he covered his feet, and with two he flew. And one cried to another and said: 'Holy, holy, holy is the Lord of hosts; The whole earth is full of His glory!'" (Isa. 6:1–3 NKJV).

The amazing thing about this angelic praise and worship is that they sing in contrast to the realities here on earth. If you notice well, Isaiah started his ministry with harsh messages of judgments because of the corruption among his people. While the prophet saw doom and gloom, the angels in the presence of the Lord looked down on the earth. All they saw was beyond the gloom darkness that besieged it. They saw God's glory.

In the presence of the Lord, we can easily learn to bypass veils of realities to see the truth. In his presence, we will understand that what is true is not the truth—that the truth is liberating, not depressing. Ruth saw the truth beyond what was true.

It could be true that your husband is acting out, or your children are not showing any progress, or that your business is heading downhill. However, remember that what is true is not the truth. The truth is the power that can change your condition, and it is only found in God. As we learn to lift our eyes above where we are, we will definitely access the truth—and our freedom will not delay.

5

Where You Die, I Will Die

This statement speaks of total commitment to the cause. Without true commitment to the cause or the vision we possess, there is no possibility to achieve them. Not only was Ruth committed, but she was loyal to Naomi even unto death. When commitment meets loyalty, there is faithfulness—and faithfulness always precedes fruitfulness. In other words, faithfulness is the sum of total commitment and loyalty.

Many start the journey, but only a handful finish. Too many give up when the going gets tough. When roads become bumpy, when the valley is too low, when the mountain is too high, they give up. Failure in the pursuit of vision and calling is not a problem of potential. It is a matter of fully being committed to what we hope to achieve. How committed are you?

This is a call to courage and the never-give-up spirit. Whatever a person begins to do with all their heart, they can truly achieve. Those who built the tower of Babel were surely on the path of success because they were committed to their enterprise. There are things that require the anointing of God upon our lives to be done; however, there are many other achievements in life that simply require courage.

As I said earlier, Joshua's requirement that the people cross over to the Promised Land called for courage. Beside his prowess to divide the Jordan River or speak to the sun and moon, God told him to be courageous. When discouragement sets in, the mighty will lose their strength.

Orpah was surely discouraged. After seeing all that she had seen and going through all those dramas, she threw in the towel and decided to change course.

Those who throw in the towel have a wrong perception of life. They assume that life is easy, and conclude that there should be no obstacles ahead. When such a mind-set takes hold, there is disconnection from our innermost strength. We spend time listening to the issues around us rather than to the voice of the vision inside.

It is a deadly affront to try to become that for which we are not willing to pay the price. The dignity of human beings is that we have been built with the capacity to rise above our obstacles. Deep within the core of our weakness is found an unlimited amount of power and strength. Through our weakness, we can find true strength and true vision. If we are truly assured that the road we have chosen is for the best and is divinely approved, then commitment to the cause will help us tap the power within us, the power of the Spirit of God to pursue, overtake, and recover.

Christ won the battle of ages in weakness when he became a man. He won the battle against the Enemy once and for all, in one blow, through the cross of his weakness. But he also had to be committed to the cause. He proved his sole commitment when he made his statement that he was ready to do the will of the Father as written in the Book (Heb. 10:7).

However, we need to know in advance that if we are contemplating throwing in the towel and calling it quits, the strength it takes to turn around and go back is far greater than the strength required to keep moving ahead.

Commitment Calls to Discipline

Discipline is the routine we create that is focused on something. Naomi knew this well. Her mistake of moving from one place to another had taught her a lesson. She told Ruth not to move to another field, but to stay committed to the field of Boaz, for such discipline would eventually pay (Ruth 2:22–23).

The application of a disciplined life is broad. We can be disciplined in our marital relationships, in business, in raising kids, and so on. Whatever we focus on doing will become our character and nature. We will then do it without thinking. Champions are disciplined for the cause. You can never break through and win in life unless you are committed and disciplined.

Commitment Is a Call to Excellence

I discovered that it is practically impossible to know our truest purpose in life unless we are passionately committed to a cause. It is not a matter of doing something, but doing everything with commitment, discipline, and passion. The thing we most ignore is that the strength it takes to turn around and go back is far greater than the strength required to keep moving ahead.

Commitment Is a Call to Focus

The correct focus is imperative. If our focus is wrong, we will end up wasting time, resources, and energy. Often, we are driven away from the real thing, the real issue that deserves our attention. Ruth's focus had to be maintained—she was there, as Naomi perceived, for Boaz. Yet there was so much possibility for her to become focused on simple gleanings and lose sight of what she was set to possess. Wrong focus creates limitations. Even though focus is needed to break through, such focus must be directed to the right cause.

Wrong Focus Creates Limitations

Most issues in life are not solved, even in marriage, because the analysis of the root of the problem or the focus on where we are trying to get is distorted. People argue over petty things and move away from the core issue that could make a difference. Discipline is the capacity to stay on course in a consistent way. Constant hammering with unbroken focus is key to breaking limitations. Walls may be thick and hard, but as we find the right spot, we keep on hammering. By staying disciplined, we will break through the wall.

6

Breaking Cycles

Another key for breaking limitations is to break the negative and even demonic cycles that revolve around our lives. Those cycles are failures, issues, pain, and temptations that come and go. Often those negative elements recur in an opportune moment. Remember what the Bible says right after the temptation of Christ: "When the devil had finished every temptation, he left Him until an opportune time" (Luke 4:13 NASB).

The opportune moments are moments when we come closer to our greatest breakthroughs—moments when we are ready to step into our truest purpose or catch a wave of blessings. That's when a negative cycle will come, trying to postpone or cancel destiny.

Ruth and the Cycle of Ancestral Spirit

Ruth had to break some cycles in her life that tied her to failure. There was a serious ancestral problem in Ruth's past that imposed restriction on moving ahead.

Remember that Ruth was a Moabite. The people of Moab had a very complicated origin.

Then Lot went up out of Zoar and dwelt in the mountains, and his two daughters were with him; for he was afraid to dwell in Zoar. And he and his two daughters dwelt in a cave. Now the firstborn said to the younger, "Our father is old, and there is no man on the earth to come in to us as is the custom of all the earth. Come, let us make our father drink wine, and we will lie with him, that we may preserve the lineage of our father." So they made their father drink wine that night. And the firstborn went in and lay with her father, and he did not know when she lay down or when she arose.

It happened on the next day that the firstborn said to the younger, "Indeed I lay with my father last night; let us make him drink wine tonight also, and you go in and lie with him, that we may preserve the lineage of our father." Then they made their father drink wine that night also. And the younger arose and lay with him, and he did not know when she lay down or when she arose.

Thus both the daughters of Lot were with
child by their father. The firstborn bore a son
and called his name Moab; he is the father of
the Moabites to this day. And the younger,
she also bore a son and called his name
Ben-Ammi; he is the father of the people of
Ammon to this day. (Gen. 19:30–38 NKJV)

Lot escaped the judgment of Sodom and Gomorrah with
his two daughters and reached the high mountain of Zoar.
Scripture shows that after a while, "there was no man in the
land," and Lot's daughters decided to preserve their family
lineage by intoxicating their father with wine and sleeping
with him. The reason for such an illicit relation was because
"there was no man" in the area. Thus, Lot's daughters turned
to their own kin to produce what they needed.

This established a mind-set. The root source of the very
existence of Moab was that when "there is no man," one
must turn to one's own kin to produce results. Moab was
established in such an evil spirit. This was one of the reasons
that the Lord forbade Moabites from entering the sanctuary
up to the tenth generation.

Ruth faced the same spirit. She was without a man. *There
was no man* indeed to help her produce a child. This was a
hidden cycle—a demonic cycle that needed to be broken. In
the spiritual realm, she was fighting with an ancestral spirit or
issue—the pressure to turn again, as did her ancestors, to her

own kin and produce needed results. This was, undoubtedly, a cycle that imposed itself and needed to be broken for Ruth to make further progress in life.

Cycles Dominant in Believers' Lives

Cycles come in many ways and many forms. Two of them are predominant in believers' lives. They are cycles of pet sins and cycles of generational curses or mistakes. These cycles present themselves every moment we make progress, with the plan of distracting and delaying our Christian walk and life achievement.

Cycles of pet sins

The writer of Hebrews warned against pet sins: "Therefore, since we have so great a cloud of witnesses surrounding us, let us also lay aside every encumbrance (weight) and the sin which so easily entangles us, and let us run with endurance the race that is set before us" (Heb. 12:1 NASB).

Scripture shows that there are cycles of unnecessary weight that can distract or hinder one from running the race of life. Those weights are not necessarily sins. Often they constitute the good things in life that get in the way of the best things God wants us to lay hold of. Pet sins can be things we usually give ourselves to, such as obsessive hobbies that steal our time and energy. They take away from our ability to concentrate on the most important assignment in life.

Usually, these sins are so entangled with us that we find no easy way to break free from them. They have become our life habits (not nature). And often the Devil will use sin habits to sidetrack us when our Kairos time approaches. Sin, as I always say, does not change God's heart and plan for us, but it does change our hearts and minds toward God. We end up missing the mark and missing what he has in store for us.

For greater advancement in life, we must break free from repetitive cycles of the same sin and same mistake. Many will agree that habits have caused us to lose relationships, jobs, opportunities, and much more. Therefore, it is of the utmost necessity that we overcome those sin habits.

One sure way we break free from pet sins is to reckon ourselves dead to sin: "Even so consider yourselves to be dead to sin, but alive to God in Christ Jesus" (Rom. 6:11 NASB). This we do when we set our eyes on Jesus Christ, not only through relationship but through fellowship. We do this by "fixing our eyes on Jesus, the Author and Perfecter of faith" (Heb. 12:2 NASB).

Earlier, Paul made it clear that "we all, with unveiled face, beholding as in a mirror the glory of the Lord, are being transformed into the same image from glory to glory, just as from the Lord, the Spirit" (2 Cor. 3:18 NKJV). We become what we behold. The power to break a sinful nature is the cross of Jesus Christ. The power to break a sin habit is in fellowshipping with him through the Holy Spirit.

Cycles of generational curses and failures

There are also demonic cycles that are generational in nature. This means that they find their root in what our forefathers have done. Often, even after salvation, these cycles seem to impose themselves in front of us. Unless we break them off, they will block our access to the place God is calling us to step into.

We have a few biblical examples of cycles or the effect of parents' sins and curses that try to find their way into our lives. In the time of Noah's flood, an entire generation of the earth suffered divine judgment for the sins of the parents (Gen 6:1–13). Ham's sin released a perpetual judgment over his descendants (Gen. 9:24–27). Achan and his whole family were judged severely by Joshua for Achan's sins (Josh. 7:24–26). Korah and his family were judged for his sinful presumption against Moses (Num. 16:23–34). Jewish children were destroyed in Jerusalem for the prior sins of adults (Luke 19:41–44).

Let me tell you something: there are many people who are blocked because of what their parents did. The effects of their parents' sin has affected many people psychologically and spiritually. Those past mistakes have become cycles because they have conditioned people to act in certain ways, thus making them failures in life. Some of those past sins have given the Devil a legal ground to manipulate and control the destiny of many.

The Price Has Been Paid—That's All You Need to Know

The issue of cycles may create the impression that the cross of Jesus has not done anything for us as far as our freedom is concerned. However, we must remember that just because Satan has been defeated on the cross does not mean that Satan has withdrawn from us forever. No, he will come as a roaring lion to discredit our freedom. He will place claims over our destiny and will try to remind us of past mistakes. Spiritually, he will try to infiltrate our freedom by imposing an illegal judgment because of what our ancestors have done. He will raise up strongholds against us, bringing cycles of pain even to the saved believer.

This is the reason many believers, even after salvation, find themselves going through the same conflicts they went through before salvation. It seems to them that their lives are still going through the same cycle. I have seen many believers struggle before and after salvation with a spiritual wife or husband. A spirit torments them at night through sexual intercourse.

The cross has fulfilled all—it has paid in full. However, such reality will transcend into our daily living only when we know it and claim it by faith.

Our ignorance of the reality of the cross is where our greatest defeat lies. So many believers are living under demonic cycles. In the life of every believer, Satan will impose these cycles at the threshold of breakthrough. You will notice that the same thing your parents suffered from, you are also undergoing.

Sometimes the fate of your community becomes your fate. The cycle can be imposed not only on a family or individual, but also on a community or a nation. When that happens, those coming out of those communities will carry the same stigma of failure. Unless the cycle is identified and broken, we will carry the same stigma even when we change the community

Our ignorance of the reality of the cross is where our greatest defeat lies.

Ruth had to face the cycle and break it. She defied the spirit that was in existence in her nation. She stretched back and defied ancestral spirits when she chose not to turn to her own kin, but to go in faith to the unknown.

Truth is, much of what the Enemy imposes on the lives of believers are illegal activities, because of our ignorance of what the cross of Jesus has done for us. We are continually paying a price while in fact this is a *tetelestai* reality—all was fulfilled. The price has been paid so that freedom can be the song we sing in our lifetimes.

There are, nevertheless, some demonic activities that are legal because of the sin we allow to have dominion over us. Yet, even when it comes to the legality of such intrusion, knowing the cross deeply and submitting to its power by faith is enough to break those acts of the Enemy over us. We were made free through the cross of Christ Jesus. When he stripped principalities and dominions and made a public spectacle over them through the cross, we were made free once and for all. And as we engage in our journey toward God's purpose, we need to proclaim the truth of the cross against any recurring cycle that may be at work against us.

Part II
Rahab's Vision

The story of Rahab is another amazing one. It shares many parallel truths with Ruth's life story. Rahab's faith has echoed throughout ages. We see it being reported later in the New Testament. She stands as a hero of faith who demonstrated that it is possible to break through any limitation and be established in a greater path. "By faith Rahab the harlot did not perish along with those who were disobedient, after she had welcomed the spies in peace" (Heb. 11:31 NASB).

James likewise describes Rahab's actions as acts of righteousness that were instrumental to securing her destiny and changing her position. "And the Scripture was fulfilled which says, 'Abraham believed God, and it was accounted to him for righteousness. And he was called the friend of God. You see then that a man is justified by works, and not by faith only. Likewise, was not Rahab the harlot also justified by works when she received the messengers and sent them out another way?'" (James 2:23–25 NKJV).

Rahab's faith touched the root of Abraham's faith. Abraham was justified by works of faith. Rahab was also justified by works of faith. Her placement in the same category with Abraham and Elijah is proof that Rahab's belief was beyond the ordinary—and thus she became an ancestor of the Lord Jesus (Matt. 1:5).

Possibility of Change

Rahab was a prostitute, yet later she was grafted into the

lineage of God the Son. She changed her position in a way that defied human logic and critics. Not only was she a prostitute, but she was a pagan woman, doomed for destruction and condemned to failure. But we see later a major change taking place because of what she believed and perceived.

Let me stress this again—she was condemned to failure because of her background. She was condemned to failure because of her lifestyle. She was condemned to failure because of her position in life. However, all that changed because she took hold of something more real than her present circumstances.

There is always something more real, more powerful— positively life-changing—amid every pain and situation we are in. There can be a way out into greater heights in life. We must have this in our minds if we would like to see great changes take place.

Rahab's story shows that where we are currently does not define our future. Many people look at their present condition as their final destination. This often accustoms them to a certain way of thinking, and they lose hope for the future. Because of that, they barely move into the possibility of greatness.

The present is what God gives us. The past is what we created. The future is the hope God has prepared for us. No one enters their future unless they learn to first embrace the present and deal with the past. Often, we forfeit the present assignment because we are more preoccupied with what happened yesterday. In that moment, the present, which is supposed to become the springboard for the future, is dislocated.

Christ describes himself as the One who is and was and is to come. "I am the Alpha and the Omega, says the Lord God, who is and was and who is to come, the Almighty" (Rev. 1:8 NASB). He starts with the present, moves to the past, and finishes with the future. Do you know how many people's lives ended in the past? This happened because they did not know how to stand in the present.

The book of Hebrews speaks of a day that remains for all of us. That day is not yesterday; that day is today. "But encourage one another day after day, as long as it is still called today, so that none of you will be hardened by the deceitfulness of sin" (Heb. 3:13 NASB). What you do today will either validate your past and harass your future, or it will silence your past and confirm your future.

Okay, what is your present condition? Where are you right now? What are the messes you are in right now? In which tower of limitations are you stationed right now? Here is the truth. Here is the good news. You can reposition yourself and be where God has destined for you to be. The possibility for positive change is unlimited. All we must do is follow the trail of Rahab to see what she did in the core of her faith and vision.

7
The Power of Your Need

It was probably a Saturday night in Jericho—yes, perhaps they had the same culture as we do today. Saturday was maybe the hottest day, when prostitutes were all over the city waiting for a moment that could allow them to make their living. Two spies entered the city. They were Israelites. One was named Salmon, and the other name we do not know.

Rahab was well stationed and she was a lucky pick of the day. These two spies, whom she welcomed into her house, were key to her change. The harlot on the tower of Jericho welcomed them, and little did she know that by doing so, she welcomed her salvation and her ticket to a better change.

But why was it that she welcomed them? Rahab would not have welcomed them unless she was a woman in need. As a prostitute, she had a tremendous sense of need. Her need was fulfilled via prostitution. Regardless of what the drive behind her need was, the point is that it was her sense of need that became the key. The reality is her need was so strong, she was burning with it—and she was open to welcoming the spies.

I do not believe that we go into the future. I believe that our future comes to us in a sequence of life events. This means that events coming into our lives carry keys to our future. Just as your future is inside of you, the same goes for events that come into your life. They are meant to connect you with your future. Everything happening around our lives is a key to connect us with the future inside of us. That is what Paul meant when he wrote that all things work together for the good (future) of those that love God (Rom. 8:28).

Those two spies were Rahab's future and they came to her. Or you could say they represented the future that was unfolding to her, and she had to seize the moment. Thank God that her sense of need was so strong. When our sense of need is shallow, we never catch the greatest moments of our lives.

The future unfolds here and there. Our connection to our future unfolds here and there. The only moment we have is the present. To reach out to our future, our sense of need must be strong. Otherwise, we will waste the meaning of every event and miss the opportunities that could change our lives.

The depth of the need is the possibility to succeed in life. Your sense of need makes you aware of things that are common and things that are uncommon. You see best and evaluate life issues best when your desires for breakthrough and great achievement are strong.

John the Baptist was one who knew the power of his need.

The gospel shows that when Christ came to the Jordan to be baptized, John said something that defined his greatness throughout eternity: "I have need to be baptized by you, and do you come to me?" (Matt. 3:14 NASB).

The power of need is crucial for shifting destiny. However, what we need and what we want in life are often different. Many desire or crave unnecessary things. Often we waste our lives pursuing what we want, leaving us empty at the end. Your need is linked to your destiny. The greater the need, the greater the passion. Your need is linked to your life vision. It is connected to what you were called to accomplish in life.

For Rahab, she needed a man, a covering. She just took the wrong path to responding to such a need. If merely sleeping with men was what she wanted, she would not have considered helping the spies. Her heart was burning for more—she wanted more than what a night in the arms of a stranger could bring. She had a deeper need to be established, her and her family. On the surface she looked bad, but on the inside there was something greater, which I believe captivated heaven.

Never judge a book by its cover. Rahab's book cover was bad. It portrayed immorality, troublemaking, and relationship-breaking. She was the enemy of pure society, and possibly had caused a lot of trouble in certain homes.

I have seen many people in our society who looked bad from the outside. Yet when heaven looks at them, it sees something more appealing than what human eyes can see.

That is the reason Christianity is filled with used-to-be-bad people. The outcasts, the troublemakers, and the failures of society are the ones God reaches out to the most. This happens because their need for salvation, for rescue, is great. When the good news is proclaimed to them, they quickly embrace it.

You see, life, with all its struggles and complexity, can be full of useful tools to reveal our deepest needs. Repositioning ourselves can never be possible unless we begin to see from the vantage point of our circumstances—the new picture we haven't seen before. Change will not come for the best unless we allow where we are to reveal what we truly need.

Every issue in life carries the seed of our truest and purest need. It just depends on how we see through those issues. Sometimes struggles reveal what we need to change or what we need to embrace.

Rahab's lowest point permitted her to see what she needed. The future came, the opportunity knocked at her door, and she grabbed it and was never the same again.

When we don't know what we need, we make the change process difficult. Ignoring why we need to change will make us superficial. Lack of knowing our truest need makes us blind and cripples our capacity to seize the opportune moment in our lives. All of us will have those moments when God will knock at the door and the miracle we have been looking for will show up. Those miracles will come in different forms. Only when we truly know what we need will we be able to benefit from those moments.

The book of Esther reveals a similar reality. Esther became queen not because she was the most beautiful woman among all the other virgins. She became queen and found greater favor because she connected to her need. She knew to set apart the difference between what she wanted and what she needed. Look at what the Bible says:

> Thus prepared, each young woman went to the king, and she was given whatever she desired to take with her from the women's quarters to the king's palace. In the evening she went, and in the morning, she returned to the second house of the women, to the custody of Shaashgaz, the king's eunuch who kept the concubines. She would not go in to the king again unless the king delighted in her and called for her by name.
>
> Now when the turn came for Esther the daughter of Abihail the uncle of Mordecai, who had taken her as his daughter, to go in to the king, she requested nothing but what Hegai the king's eunuch, the custodian of the women, advised. And Esther obtained favor in the sight of all who saw her. So Esther was taken to King Ahasuerus, into his royal palace,

in the tenth month, which is the month of Tebeth, in the seventh year of his reign. The king loved Esther more than all the other women, and she obtained grace and favor in his sight more than all the virgins; so he set the royal crown upon her head and made her queen instead of Vashti. (Esther 2:13–17 NKJV)

Each young woman had her turn. As they were at the face of their future, they were asked to take whatever they desired. And so they did. Each one had her time, her pivotal moment to seize greatness in life.

In her time, Esther did not go with what she wanted. She chose nothing but what the wisdom of Hegai revealed. That was the decisive point in her life. It came down to choosing. Our choices, like Esther's, will be influenced by what drives our innermost being—the power of want or the power of need.

Remember, every life issue, negative or positive, contains the seed of truest destiny—need. In the same way that beauty came through chaos, so our destiny is forged through the fire of many combined issues. Those pains help set the line of separation between human want and human-divine need.

8

The Power of a Transformed Mind

Another fascinating point is that Rahab changed her mind. As a prostitute, her mind was bent to thinking in a certain way. Men who entered her house were for games, not for serious relationships. However, something changed in her mind. She received two spies who could have been some great saving for her. She decided that this time, the opportunity would be for a change in her life. Her mind was transformed, no longer thinking like a prostitute. She saw in her new mind the big picture heaven had for her.

She was limited in her mind. The way she perceived life, the way she saw men coming and going, was set in one way. For change to take place and for a break to occur in her limitation, she had to change her way of thinking.

The ultimate key for repositioning ourselves or changing our lives for the best is in our minds. No one goes where one's mind has not reached. In fact, we are the product of our minds. Your life is the sum of what rules your mind. "For as he thinks in his heart, so is he" (Prov. 23:7 NKJV).

Before we change the direction of our lives, we must change the streams flowing in our minds. We do not perceive life through our natural eyes. Eyes are the windows of our souls. True perception is from your mind, and the quality of your life is decided within that sphere.

Your mind is prophetic of your future. It forecasts with perfect detail what will happen in your life. It is very easy to foretell where you will end up—simply look at what you think about. Your inner thought prophesies continually about your destiny. You cannot escape the fate of your mind-set. You are so intertwined with it that wherever your mind goes, there you will also go. Where your mind limits itself is your limitation. The horizon your mind does not perceive, you will never perceive either.

Rahab had to shift her mind and see more than simple customers in those two spies. She had to exercise her mind to see beyond Jericho's wall and find another wall of security— the God of Israel. Her mind became the ultimate key for breaking her limitations.

Your Mind Is Prophetic of Your Future

To shift destiny, we need to learn how to change our thinking. Spiritually speaking, the transformation of the mind is crucial. The apostle Paul evokes something very profound: "And do not be conformed to this world, but be transformed by the renewing of your mind, that you may prove what is that good and acceptable and perfect will of God" (Rom. 12:2 NKJV).

The term *world* here denotes vanity, meaning things that do not contribute to a better future. The renewing of the mind is the only referee that approves God's perfect will for life. His will is relevant, deep, and beautiful for us. He wants us to live heaven on earth, to prosper, and to succeed in all we do. However, only to the degree that we allow our minds to be renewed will we be able to appreciate and embrace such will.

The renewing of the mind is the source of peace. "You will keep him in perfect peace, whose mind is stayed on You, because he trusts in You" (Isa. 26:3 NKJV).

The peace that proceeds from setting our mind on the Lord surpasses all understanding. "Be anxious for nothing, but in everything by prayer and supplication, with thanksgiving, let your requests be made known to God; and the peace of God, which surpasses all understanding, will guard your hearts and minds through Christ Jesus" (Phil. 4:6–7 NKJV).

It should be noted that the key that Isaiah spoke, regarding setting our minds on the Lord, is well expounded here in the epistle to the Philippians. We keep our mind on the Lord when, through every life circumstance, we present our case before God through prayer, supplication, and thanksgiving. Through this process, we find peace and clarity to see the issues of life with divine perspective.

The moment Rahab decided to embrace another mind-set was the moment a door to the future was opened. How is your mind? How are you thinking? If the same old thoughts brought you into the mess you are presently in, I suggest you embrace another thought.

I discover that sometimes, God graciously allows issues of life to come against us to help change our way of thinking. Our weakness resurfaces from time to time to allow us to embrace another mind-set.

On another note, the Lord will do wonders here and there in our lives, giving us small breakthroughs so that our minds will no longer be subject to the limitation of mere human beings, but will rise to thinking like Christ.

Embracing the Mind of Christ

Christ Jesus lived with a different mind-set. He was a man who had many oppositions in life—death threats hanging on his neck, enemies everywhere. On top of all that, he lived with the knowledge of his tragic death on the horizon. Yet Christ walked in perfect peace and fulfilled his destiny to the fullest. The key was his mind—he knew how to set his mind on God.

Such is what the renewing of our minds leads to. A positive way of thinking about life is not enough. Though that is beautiful, God has given us the opportunity to attain, if I may say, the highest mind that ever lived and is still active—the mind of Christ. By right of redemption, we do not just have access to the mind of Christ. Even more, we *possess* the mind of Christ. "For who has known the mind of the Lord that he may instruct Him? But we have the mind of Christ" (1 Cor. 2:16 NKJV).

The way I see it, Christ came on earth and lived a pure life. He was tempted in every way possible, like all of us (Heb. 4:15). His mind registered all the oppositions, difficulties, and strategies for winning in life. After his resurrection, he became a Spirit-giving life when he came to live inside of us (1 Cor. 15:45). He downloaded his mind on us. That download contains all the experiences, fight, opposition, and strategies for winning in life. We have the mind of Christ. We have the key to a glorious life. We have what it takes to break every limitation in life.

Having the mind of Christ is not a religious thing, for it does not suggest the exclusion of secular things. It means possessing the perfect design for living. It means that as we engage in life's issues—doing business, pursuing careers—we are so tuned in with the heartbeat of God that we think in alignment with God, knowing how he would have done what we are doing right now.

God created everything. He is the author of science. Therefore, he expects us to also be creative. The mind of Christ in this case means that now I am so transformed that I seek for God to be glorified in all that I do. All that I do in my life, I do unto God, not unto man.

God is not disconnected from our reality. This is a truth we all need to know and replay repeatedly in our minds. God is interested to the details of our lives in a way that we cannot comprehend, for he is a good God. He never came into our existence for the sake only of saving our spirits. God is interested in our life endeavors. In fact, God loves your business more than you love it. He loves raising your kids for a better future more than you do. He loves plants more than those who study them. And so on. This makes him want to collaborate with us so that he will share the load of our daily routine.

However, when our minds become self-centered, we lose the privilege to walk and work with the divine. We limit our possibility of rising to our highest potential. The renewed mind begins to see what others do not see. It is a mind turned to God, to walk with him and work with him. It is a mind that seeks to implement the will of God in every life issue. It imposes such will in every venue of human activity.

The Word of God or the Good Report

The tool for renewing our minds is the Word of God. But was Rahab a student of the Word? Though not clearly stated, it does seem that the good report of what God had done for Israel changed Rahab's mind. Remember that she told the spies something that became the bedrock of her faith.

Now before they lay down, she came up to them on the roof, and said to the men: "I know that the Lord has given you the land, that the terror of you has fallen on us, and that all the inhabitants of the land are fainthearted because of you. For we have heard how the Lord dried up the water of the Red Sea for you when you came out of Egypt, and what you did to the two kings of the Amorites who were on the other side of the Jordan, Sihon and Og, whom you utterly destroyed. And as soon as we heard these things, our hearts melted; neither did there remain any more courage in anyone because of you, for the Lord your God, He is God in heaven above and on earth beneath. Now therefore, I beg you, swear to me by the Lord, since I have shown you kindness, that you also will show kindness to my father's house, and give me a true token, and spare my father, my mother, my brothers, my sisters, and all that they have, and deliver our lives from death." (Josh. 2:8–13 NKJV)

Rahab used the words "for we have heard." Faith comes from what we hear from the Word of Christ (Rom. 10:17). Such truth of God's exploits reframed Rahab's mind. She received revelation knowledge that God was God in heaven above and on earth beneath. She was able, therefore, to see small men in giants, and great warriors in small men. The size of the sons of Anak, keepers of the gate of Jericho, did not matter anymore.

Many years back, the Israelites trembled at the report of the twelve spies. The people who saw miracles and great victories displayed did not believe. But this woman, who never saw any of those things—simply heard—had tremendous faith to believe that Israel would possess Canaan. Her faith was so strong through the renewing of her mind that she did not fear the threat of death. Once she set her eyes on a possibility of change, there was no second thought. She refused to be double-minded or to review her decision. For Rahab, that was the ultimate: the good and great report of the God of Israel renewed her mind.

If we feed our minds with the Word of life, which is the Word *for* life, then we will daily see a transformation, a metamorphosis taking place to the point that we will rightly think about life issues. We will therefore discover God's will in everything we do in life. Our ability to express his heartbeat will be unprecedented. Through her willingness to change the course of her mind, Rahab became one of the ultimate recipients through which Christ would come into the world (Matt. 1:5).

There are greater purposes of God attached to our existence. They will be expressed in different venues: some in business, some in medicine, some in sports, some in religious work, and many others. Regardless of the venue, we are all designed to express the greater purposes of God. However, it will require a transformed mind to truly live such a divine design for our existence.

The Power of Divine Acts for the Renewal of the Mind

God changes our minds through his acts. Every divine act in our lives is not meant simply for celebration. God designs those acts to change the way we view life. They are for the renewing of our minds. If we lose consciousness of what God is doing in our lives or of what God did yesterday, our minds will remain unrenewed and we will not unleash our power to break through obstacles.

The book of Mark shows something very interesting. As you read Mark 6:33–52, you'll see that Jesus preached the gospel to five thousand men, not counting women and children. The people became hungry, and the disciples proposed to Jesus that he send them away. Jesus challenged the disciples, telling them to provide food for the people. The disciples said that there was no way to find enough food to feed such a crowd. Even the five loaves and two fishes brought forward were not enough. Jesus multiplied the bread in front of them, feeding everyone, with twelve baskets left over.

Later that evening, Jesus came to his disciples, walking on water. They were afraid, and yet Jesus entered the boat with them. Scripture underlines a very deep truth: the disciples were afraid because they had not gained insight from the miracles of loaves and fishes. The miracle was meant to give them insight into the possibilities of Christ and, in consequence, change their ways of thinking.

A few days later, Christ preached the gospel to fewer people than before. This time the crowd numbered four thousand (Mark 8:1–8). The disciples were faced with the same dilemma—the people were hungry, and there was not enough bread to feed them. The Lord challenged the disciples again. Astonishingly, the same disciples, facing the same problem with the same Jesus, fell into the same folly. They asked again, "Where will we find enough bread for this crowd?"

Were they not there when Christ performed the first miracle of the loaves and fishes? Why did they respond the same way? It was because they did not allow the miracle to change their minds. They forgot quickly about what Christ had done yesterday.

The point is, we need to gain insight into what God is doing in our lives and in the lives of others. God intends, behind all his acts, to renew our way of thinking so that we see life in a different way. Remembering that divine acts are tools to reshape our thinking.

9

The Power of Your Weakness

Rahab's weakness was a magnet of favor. If she had been a woman of status, she would not have received the spies. If she had been a strong woman, she would not have had need of the spies. Her future changed because she was a woman in weakness. Her weakness became one of the main keys for ushering her into a greater future. What seemed to be a disadvantage was used for her advantage. It was her weakness that created a path for change. While people beat themselves up for their weaknesses, God's power is made perfect in weakness (2 Cor. 12:9).

God the Son came to us in weakness. He has sent deliverers repeatedly because of human weaknesses. By no means is God against us because we are weak. The thing God despises the most is when a person glories in their strength instead of in their weakness (2 Cor. 12:10). God longs to use our weaknesses to display his power.

I am not by any means stating that we should glorify immorality. However, I am looking at the principle behind

Rahab's immorality. I consider such an issue a weakness in principle.

Power Made Perfect in Weakness

Weakness is our vulnerable point. It is also a place where God allows us to be overwhelmed for the perfect purpose of his will. Paul, when arrested and in prison, did not know why he was limited. He was in a state of weakness. However, he noticed that whatever happened to him served for the furtherance of the gospel, so that the gospel reached the high corridors of Rome's systems (Phil. 1:12–14).

Your weakness is not your limitation, whether it is a habit you are struggling with or a lack of certain qualities. What seems to be a disadvantage can become an advantage for you. Our limits can easily become our beginnings in God. This is another way of stating that when we are weak, it is then that we are strong. Though we might be still in a state of weakness, this state is also a state of strength.

I truly believe that on earth, no person is at a disadvantage to others if they know how to use their weakness well. No person is behind any other person. Your weakness does not put you behind others who seem to be stronger. You have the same opportunity as they do to rise and break through in life. Look around your weakness or through your weakness—you will see a strength attached to it.

The mistake most people make is that they try to see

themselves through the lens of other people's potential. I compare myself to him or to her to measure my potential. Such an attempt can be costly to one's destiny.

Often, we take such an approach in life because of the weaknesses that beset us. Too many people live in regret because of areas in which they do not seem to have strength. However, we need to understand that by no means is our weakness a curse. In fact, I believe that weakness is the base attraction of God's grace, especially if we know how to humble ourselves before God.

Samson was able to kill more Philistines when he reached the stage of weakness. When he was strong, he had small victories here and there. But in the highest state of weakness, he was able to tap into greater power and kill more Philistines in a day than he had in his lifetime. Our greatest power lies in knowing our weaknesses.

Rahab's Strength Hidden in Her Weakness

Rahab the harlot had a tremendous weakness. Well, she was a harlot! Yet, though she displayed little moral virtue, there was a strength that developed in the same spot as her weakness. As a harlot, she was more social than many people. Her level of hospitality rose to a higher place. The weakness of harlotry that controlled her life was used by God to develop a capacity that made her receptive to divine grace. I strongly believe that the Devil did not see that one coming.

God is not absent from the life of any being on earth. He works in the life of every human being to create a door of hope amid the seeming disadvantages that surface in human lives. Every demonic work against us, any flaw we have in our lives creates a vacuum for God's ultimate purpose to be fulfilled. The God who works all things for our good can use downfall, shortcomings, and weakness to create a breakthrough. His capacity to bring hope out of desperate situations is unparalleled. God knows how to outplay the plans of the Devil, how to use the Devil's evil plans to advance God's good plans, and how to use the negatives in our lives to create in us the perfect image he intends for us to reflect. Thus, God could take the church persecutor, Saul, and make out of him the greatest apostle in the church.

Every demonic work against us and every flaw we have create voids for God's ultimate purpose to enter and be fulfilled. It only depends on how we approach God for grace.

I Glory in My Weakness

To know our weakness is wisdom. Great generals don't perish because of their weaknesses but because of their strengths. Wise men glory in their weaknesses, for in doing so, we supply our strengths with perfect power to be more efficient. A person who knows their weaknesses and limitations knows how to set boundaries. Therefore, it is very difficult for such a person to stumble easily.

Knowledge of one's weakness does not suggest low self-esteem. These are two different things. Low self-esteem exists when someone has a general feeling of insignificance or a lack of importance. What I am talking is different. Knowing our worth, importance, and significance in Christ, we do not glory in them. But while maintaining our knowledge of these truths, we glory in the area of our weakness, for such will be a safeguard against falling and crashing in life. True humility, which is the great recipient of all divine grace and favor, glories not in strength, but rather in weakness. This is the wisdom that Paul found later in his life. "And He said to me, 'My grace is sufficient for you, for My strength is made perfect in weakness.' Therefore, most gladly I will rather boast in my infirmities, that the power of Christ may rest upon me" (2 Cor. 12:9 NKJV).

We are not limited by knowing our limitations. Such knowledge, when properly managed, will permit us to supply ourselves with what we lack. In that moment, in the very place where we were limited, we find a key to advance to a place of greater knowledge and greater power.

The mistake some people make is that they think their limitations and weaknesses are clear indications that they will never get better in those areas. Thus, they excuse themselves even when grace (the two spies) knocks at the door. However, a person can learn any craft. We just need to be disciplined and put all our passion into whatever it is we want to improve upon. We can do all things through Christ who strengthens us.

Our weaknesses do not alienate us from success and breakthrough in life. The life of Rahab showed that we can move from being bystanders on the road into engaging in the journey of life. There is a grace available for the weak and a mercy for the downcast. We can surely do all things through Christ who strengthens us.

You are not entirely weak. If you look intently, you will see that God has endowed you with certain qualities with which you can climb higher mountains.

10
Breaking the Cycle

Rahab could not exit her present place and access destiny unless she broke the cycle that was repetitive in her life. As we saw in the story of Ruth, when we engage for breakthrough, we have to deal with our past issues. We stand in the present. Yet as we seek to embrace and walk in the future, often the past comes to visit. That is why Christ introduced himself as the One who is and was and is to come, placing the past between the present and the future (Rev. 1:8).

When the past revisits us, it comes in the form of what we call *cycles*. These are spirits, past failures, past weaknesses, or things we gave up long ago that come around in times of breakthrough.

Put another way, a cycle is an ongoing issue that stands as a stronghold in a person's life, making that person an object of failure in a certain area. Rahab had the cycle of prostitution—this was a stronghold in her life. It surely was not easy for her. I believe at the moment the spies came knocking, her temptation was great. The cycle was restarted, and she probably felt the desire rising to sleep with these two Israelites. She had to choose between satisfying her fleshly desire or embracing a greater destiny. She had to submit to the cycle that had made her a failure or choose something much more valuable—an inheritance with God's people in the light. The cycle in your life must be identified and broken for breakthrough to be possible.

This is a reality seen in many places in the Bible. In Judges chapter 6, there is an interesting element in the conflict between Israel and Midian. Israel suffered a continuous cycle during the harvest time because of Midian. "So it was, whenever Israel had sown, Midianites would come up; also Amalekites and the people of the East would come up against them. Then they would encamp against them and destroy the produce of the earth as far as Gaza, and leave no sustenance for Israel, neither sheep nor ox nor donkey" (Judg. 6:3–4 NKJV). Midian waited till the opportune moment before they rose against Israel. For Israel, this was a demonic cycle that kept coming back and stealing their blessings.

These demonic cycles are rampant in the lives of many people. I've met a lot of people going through these cycles. Some suffer cycles of financial struggle. Whenever money comes in, they experience the same kind of problem that robs them of the opportunity to enjoy their blessings. These cycles are demonic and well programmed by the Enemy to delay and cancel breakthrough.

Source of Struggles

Not every human struggle nor every obstacle is demonic in nature. Struggles and obstacles have diverse sources.

Human mistakes can cause some struggles and obstacles. Our lack of knowledge and good judgment can cause delay and put us in great difficulty. Breakthrough can only come when we adjust our thinking and take actions that are relevant to change the course of things. We cannot wait on God to fix what is within our sphere of control. We need divine wisdom to help us control what we need to control.

Divine providence can also cause some obstacles and afflictions. This is what God does in his own authority for a sovereign purpose. He engineers circumstances sometimes to break us, make us, transform us, or even further his plan and purpose on earth. These afflictions are not usually meant to last forever. In this case, we need faith and trust in him.

Here we have the example of Hannah. She was barren. Her situation had its source in God, for the Bible clearly shows that the Lord was the One who closed her womb (1 Sam. 1:5). Similarly, Abraham's struggle to have a child was not a satanic work, but simply something connected to God's timing and plan. In such cases, we are required to be still in prayer and worship and wait for the timing of God to be perfect.

Satanic assaults can also cause struggles and obstacles. This is where we see demonic cycles, ancestral spirits, and generational curses overtaking people's lives and subduing them into misery. Without the proper knowledge of our right in Christ through the blood of Jesus and the knowledge of our authority in Christ, we will continue to live under curses for which the price has already been paid. Breaking those cycles in the power of the name of Jesus and decreeing our freedom through the blood of Jesus is inevitable.

The cycle must be broken at once through repentance from dead works. It must be broken through choosing the way God is showing us, even though it may not present much hope at first view. We must use the authority of the name of the Lord over those cycles.

Rahab repented that very day, and the cycle was broken. Temptation was no longer strong enough to keep her conditioned to yesterday's limitations. She was free to embrace a new way and a new path.

However, we must remember that this part of breaking cycles is made easier to the degree that our minds have been renewed. The renewal of the mind is the ultimate key to deeper deliverance. We will not experience the fullness of our freedom until our minds are completely free. In fact, that is what repentance means—the change of mind. Our acts of repentance remove from the Devil the legal ground to harass our lives.

Many who came out of Egypt died, not at the hand of the Enemy, but in the hands of God himself. Why? Because they refused to let go of Egypt in their minds. Only two, Joshua and Caleb, were of a different spirit and entered the Promised Land. I believe that the expression "different spirit" is equivalent to the New Testament term "renewed mind."

11

The Spirit of Faith

Now before they lay down, she came up to them on the roof, and said to the men: "I know that the Lord has given you the land, that the terror of you has fallen on us, and that all the inhabitants of the land are fainthearted because of you. For we have heard how the Lord dried up the water of the Red Sea for you when you came out of Egypt, and what you did to the two kings of the Amorites who were on the other side of the Jordan, Sihon and Og, whom you utterly destroyed. And as soon as we heard these things, our hearts melted; neither did there remain any more courage in anyone because of you, for the Lord your God, He is God in heaven above and on earth beneath. Now therefore, I beg you, swear to me by the Lord, since I have shown you kindness, that you also will show kindness to my father's house, and give me a true token, and spare my father, my mother, my brothers, my sisters, and all that they have, and deliver our lives from death." (Josh. 2:8–13 NKJV)

Rahab was a woman of tremendous faith, and according to James, she proved that faith goes alongside with works. Her statement and kind act toward the spies were a demonstration of the Spirit of faith.

Was not Abraham our father justified by works when he offered Isaac his son on the altar? Do you see that faith was working together with his works, and by works faith was made perfect? And the Scripture was fulfilled which says, "Abraham believed God, and it was accounted to him for righteousness." And he was called the friend of God. You see then that a man is justified by works, and not by faith only. Likewise, was not Rahab the harlot also justified by works when she received the messengers and sent them out another way? For as the body without the spirit is dead, so faith without works is dead also. (James 2:21–26 NKJV)

Before I go further, I would like to show you the constituent of the Spirit of faith of which Paul referred (2 Cor. 4:13). There are five constituents that make the Spirit of faith:

1. hearing the Word of Christ—the revealed Word of Christ
2. believing the Word of promise
3. declaring the Word of faith
4. working out one's faith
5. obeying divine instructions in the waiting moment

Rahab exhibited all these qualities of the Spirit of faith. As stated in Scripture, she heard of the wonders the God of Israel displayed. She believed without seeing. She declared to the spies her faith that God was all powerful, for nothing is possessed in the kingdom of God or even in life unless there is a declaration. Our words have the power to create—in fact, the word of *faith* creates everything. Rahab also was obedient when given instruction in how to secure her salvation. She was asked to place a scarlet thread on the window of her house, and she obeyed (Josh. 2:21).

Rahab then did something that is the capstone of the true Spirit of faith—she proved her faith through works. It is in this dimension that she is mentioned in the book of James. Breakthrough requires faith with works. This has been the dividing point between believers who succeed and those who do not.

Rahab's works of faith were more than moral. She had the commitment to prove what she believed. True faith is made perfect, as James shows, through works. The Greek word we translate as "perfect" is *teleioo*. According to *The Analytical*

Greek Lexicon, it means "to execute fully; discharge; to reach the end of; run through; finish; to consummate; place in a condition of finality; to be brought to the goal; to reach the end of one's course; to be fully developed."

When we believe in the possibilities of something, we prove it by working it out. The proof that one has faith transcends simple declaration—it touches works. Rahab was not justified by her moral standard. Instead, she was justified because she acted on what she believed. Her belief in the God of Israel prompted her to receive the spies. At the risk of her life, she hid them, despite the threat of the king. She also interceded for her life and her family's lives to be spared, because she believed that Israel had already won the war.

There are many who believe in the possibility of a better life, better marriage, better career, and so on. Yet their faith is not made complete because they have never stepped out of their comfort zone to work out what they have seen. Often, breakthrough is hindered not because of a demonic activity at work, but simply because there are no works following our faith. You cannot walk on water unless you step out of the boat.

If you believe in what you believe, what do you do about it? Are you working toward the thing you perceive by faith? Faith is not passive; it is always active. Abraham received the promise for Canaan. The next thing the Bible teaches us is that he stepped out and journeyed toward Canaan. Between where we are and where we want to go, the missing link is the proven works of faith.

Faith without works is dead. This means that works are the lifeline of faith. Many people talk about what they believe is possible for them to become and achieve. Yet only a few truly take action toward those perceived realities. And that is where many are still trapped in mediocrity.

Risk Takers

Rahab could not have broken through life's limitations unless she faced fear and the threat of soldiers (Josh. 2:3–4). She defied the king's order by hiding the spies. She was not afraid of anything—she took a tremendous risk. Life's greatest achievements are not possible without taking risks. In fact, true faith involves taking risks.

Our fear of failure is one of the greatest barriers of limitation. Risk takers are breakers—those who are not afraid to step out of the ordinary to try something extraordinary. God has created us to be great. That is what the blessings of Abraham grant to each one of us. However, the law of faith shows that there must be some risks before we step into our truest divine destiny.

The redemption of mankind was a great risk God took. If Christ had succumbed, even for a moment, to human weaknesses of sin and unrighteousness, then God would have been forever corrupted and the whole universe would have come to an end. Everything that is would have stopped being.

Both Rahab and Ruth were risk takers. They were not afraid of the unknown. They were not afraid of the new. They were not afraid of tomorrow. When the season came, they moved with God through the issues they were facing. The faith of Rahab defied everything around her. She was not afraid of confrontation to get the best she wanted.

Delivered from Darkness yet Enslaved by Fear

One of the deadliest barriers is fear. In fact, the scheme of the enemy is such that after the Lord has delivered many believers from the devil's realm, he sends fear to control our life.

"Inasmuch then as the children have partaken of flesh and blood, He Himself likewise shared in the same, that through death He might destroy him who had the power of death, that is, the devil, and release those who through fear of death were all their lifetime subject to bondage" (Heb. 2:14–15 NKJV). In this passage of Scripture, we see two works of Christ releasing us into our abundant life. Christ first deals with the Devil—the one who has the power of death—and destroys him. The Devil was "destroyed." That is some serious word, "destroy." Perhaps many of us have not understood that on the cross, Jesus did not just overcome the Devil or beat him up—he destroyed the guy. It was total annihilation of the Devil.

The Devil was rendered idle, inactive, inoperative. He lost all efficiency. He was deprived of power.

After the annihilation of the Devil, Christ deals with another element that the Enemy uses to control those for whom Christ has died—the element of fear. Once fear sets in, it empowers the Devil to control our lives, while in fact he has already lost the authority to do so. Since he cannot control us by authority, he does so by fear.

Sadly, many believers are living in fear. I have met those who, after being delivered from lifelong battles with forces of darkness, build a mechanism of fear. What they have gone through has left such a mark on them that they carry a stigma and hibernate in fear. Fear is as deadly as the Devil in authority. Christ has not given us into bondage to a spirit of fear. "For God has not given us a spirit of fear, but of power and of love and of a sound mind" (2 Tim. 1:7 NKJV).

Every great breakthrough requires that we face our deadliest enemy, and in this case, the enemy is fear. Fear of the past, fear of the present, fear of the future, fear of failures, fear of being misunderstood, fear that my age is advanced and I am not married nor have children—any kind of fear must be faced and replaced with hope.

Rahab could easily have fallen into fear of the soldiers that knocked on her door. She could have betrayed the spies. But she never allowed fear to control her for even one moment.

She stood her ground, even if the order came from the throne itself. She believed in the highest throne that sent these spies—the everlasting throne of God. For we only overcome by the blood of the Lamb, by the words of our testimonies, and by overcoming the fear of death (Rev. 12:11). The fearless ones are the breakers of limitations.

It is not the enemy who kills us— it is the *fear* of the enemy that paralyzes and kills us. Fear is like the web of the Enemy; once caught in it, we lose motion. The simplest things in life can easily sway us and create obstacles and limitations on our journey.

The Enemy has no power over us. We have both power and authority, more than he does. What he does is to send fear. Once fear sets in, discouragement finds its way, and then the Enemy can easily move into our territory and do damage. We will be surprised, when we move to the other side of eternity on the day of judgment, to find out how small and powerless was the Devil who troubled our lives and existences.

Jesus says, "Fear not, for I am with you" (Isa. 41:10 NKJV). The One who is with us is greater than the one who is in this world. Once such hope fills our hearts, we will triumphantly face life with all its mountains and obstacles. Guess what? At the end of the day, we will break through any limitation.